A book from Parables4Kids!

Copyright © 2024 Parables4Kids.com
All rights reserved.

Copyright © 2024 Jeffrey T. Small and Aldous Lux

All rights reserved. No part of this book may be reproduced in any form without permission from the authors, except as permitted by U.S. copyright law.

To request permission, contact jeff@parables4kids.com.

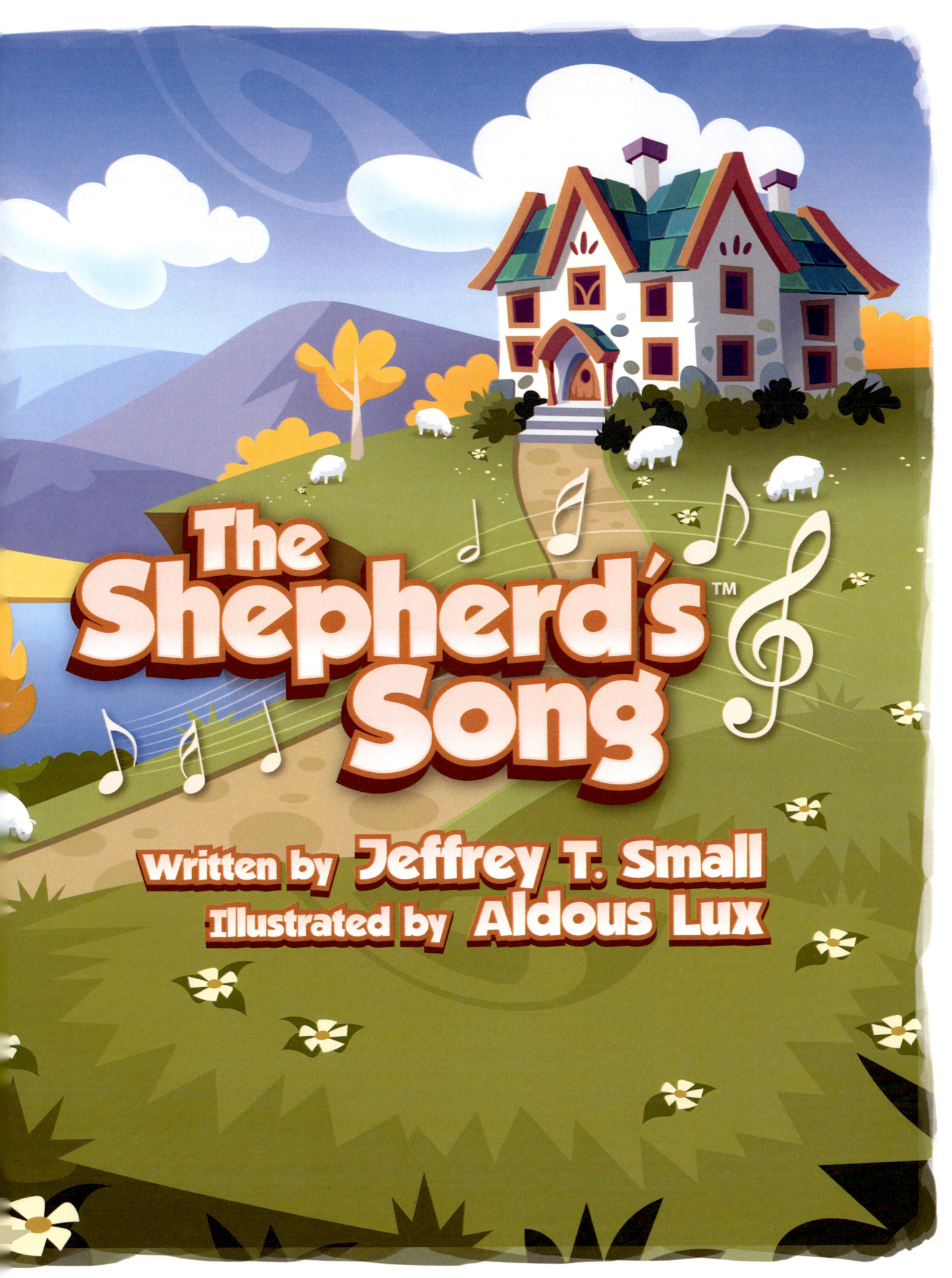

Chapter 1
The Great Shepherd

There once was a Great Shepherd who lived in a beautiful house nestled amidst majestic mountains overlooking a tranquil lake. His vast domain teemed with many creatures, including horses, cows, chickens, pigs, and even llamas!

Each morning the Great Shepherd embarked on a stroll through his picturesque land, tenderly offering greetings to all of his creatures. As a gesture of his kindness, he provided them with nourishment and gave each one of them gentle pats or scratches behind their ears. The Shepherd loved all his animals; however, he had a special love reserved for his beloved sheep.

The Shepherd's love for his sheep was profound; he knew each one by name, having been present at their births and comforting them in their passing. Whether lost or ailing, he spared no effort in tending to their needs. If one got lost, he would search for it until it was found. If one was sick, he would be near it until it was better. He protected the sheep from the wolves and other predators that would try and eat them.

There was nothing the Shepherd would not do for his sheep. This is what made him a Great Shepherd. He loved his sheep and enjoyed spending time with them. Each morning he would walk his flock to a large field where other shepherds brought their sheep. The sheep would eat to their hearts' content under the vigilant gaze of their caretaker.

As the day drew to a close, he would sing a song to gather all his sheep together before bringing them back home:

"Gentle flock, hear my song,
Your Shepherd calls you home.
Time for rest, my dearest ones,
No more these fields you roam.
Join my fold, let worries cease.
I'll lead you to the haven of peace.
Precious flock, hear my voice.
Come and follow me."

Each day the Great Shepherd would sing this song, and every day his sheep heard his voice, stopped what they were doing, and followed the Shepherd as he led them back home. Day by day, week by week, year by year, this was the routine.

Chapter 2
The Shepherd's Commission

One day the Shepherd called for his most trusted servants, John and Jacob. He told them that he needed to go away on an important journey. During his absence, he entrusted the care of his home; gardens; and cherished animals, with a special emphasis on his beloved sheep, to the two men. The Shepherd handed the keys to his home to his servants along with some money for supplies.

"I must go find a bigger piece of land that we can move to. Take care of my home, my gardens, and all my animals, especially my sheep, for I love them most. Bring them to the fields each day so they can eat. When it is time to return home, just sing this song..."

"Gentle flock, hear my song,
Your Shepherd calls you home.
Time for rest, my dearest ones,
No more these fields you roam.
Join my fold, let worries cease.
I'll lead you to the haven of peace.
Precious flock, hear my voice.
Come and follow me."

He told his trusted servants, "Sing it, word for word, and when my sheep hear it they will come."

The men asked, "How long will you be gone?"

The Shepherd answered, "I cannot predict the day or time, but I give you my word that I will return. If you prove faithful in safeguarding my flock, a reward awaits you."

The three men walked to the rustic barn where the sheep were waking from their sleep. The Shepherd took one last look at his flock which he knew he would miss dearly. He turned to his servants and embraced each man warmly before giving one last instruction.

"Should any of my sheep escape or become lost, remember to sing my song, and they will return to you."

With that, the Shepherd turned and began his lengthy journey down the dirt road, leading away from his cherished home.

Chapter 3
The Great Storm

Day by day, the two servants were faithful to the commands of their master. They tended to the house and all the animals on the farm, paying close attention to the Shepherd's beloved sheep. Every day they led the sheep to their pasture and kept a careful eye on them as they feasted on the luscious emerald grass.

One fateful day, as the two servants were watching diligently over the vast land of grazing sheep, a great storm arrived. It covered the entirety of the land the Shepherd and his sheep lived on. Violent winds, booming thunder, relentless lightning, and blackened skies quickly blanketed the land.

The sheep, gripped by fear, ran frantically in all directions from their grazing grounds. In the chaos, many ventured so far from their field that the familiar path home eluded them.

Amid the tumult, opportunistic thieves came and stole many of the sheep, taking them far away from their secure home. Wolves, also taking advantage of the unprotected flock, pursued the scattered sheep, driving those that fled into the depths of the forests.

When the storm finally subsided, the two servants surveyed the aftermath, only to discover the disheartening absence of every last one of the sheep. The once peaceful flock, contentedly grazing in their fields, now found themselves dispersed far and wide across the vast expanse of unknown lands.

Chapter 4
The Servants' Mission

Deep sorrow and heavy anxiety filled the hearts of the servants.

Jacob turned to John and asked, "What shall we do? The Shepherd loves his sheep and if he returns and finds them scattered, he will be both sorrowful at his loss and angry with us."

John replied, "We need to go out into the land and find his sheep."

Jacob responded skeptically, "There are so many sheep throughout all the land. How can we possibly know which ones are his?"

With conviction, John explained, "Remember what the Shepherd told us. We must sing the Shepherd's song, for when we do, his sheep will hear it, know it, and follow us."

John added, "We must go quickly, for we do not know when the master of the house will return."

Armed with determination, the two men gathered necessary supplies and embarked on the quest to reclaim the lost sheep.

John set out toward the east, while Jacob ventured in the opposite direction to the west.

Chapter 5
The Servants' Challenge

On the first day of their mission, John came across a herd of sheep in a field. He stood on the edge of the field and sang the Shepherd's song with resounding clarity. Immediately, a few dozen sheep ceased their activities and ran towards him. They gathered around John and followed him as he continued walking down the path to the next field.

Town by town, field by field, John would find a group of sheep and sing the Shepherd's song. Sometimes many sheep heard it and responded to it, while other times, sadly, none recognized its familiar tune. Occasionally, some sheep would start to follow but then veer off to explore other preferred fields. These, however, were not the Shepherd's sheep.

Despite the outcome, John steadfastly adhered to the Shepherd's command, faithfully trusting and obeying that the Shepherd's sheep would hear his song and follow.

Meanwhile, the second servant, Jacob, journeyed westward and likewise encountered a flock of sheep.

Following the Shepherd's instructions, he too sang his song, and just as the Shepherd told him, some sheep heard the melody and followed him.

However, as he went town by town and field by field singing the Shepherd's song, not many sheep responded. This frustrated and discouraged him. He really wanted to find as many sheep as he could and please the Shepherd. Driven by this desire, he thought of a new strategy. Instead of just singing the Shepherd's song, he bought vegetables and grains to entice the sheep so they would follow him.

The next day Jacob stood on the edge of a field where sheep were grazing. He sang the Shepherd's song and, as expected, only one or two sheep responded. Then he reached into his satchel and pulled out a large bag of grain.

Holding it up in the air, he shook it and called out, "Come follow me, sheep, and I will give you all the grain you can eat!"

His new strategy was successful! Instead of just a handful of sheep approaching, a substantial number eagerly accepted his offer of grains and chose to follow him. He knew these were not the Shepherd's original flock, but he didn't care. His sole purpose now was to bring back as many sheep as possible by any means necessary. Before long, he found himself accompanied by a procession of hundreds of sheep, firmly believing that this enlarged flock would undoubtedly bring satisfaction to the Shepherd.

Chapter 6
The Return Of The Sheep

After a long period of traveling throughout the entire land, the two servants returned with the sheep to the Shepherd's home.

John brought back many sheep who all gathered in their stalls, knowing they were home. They knew the look of their stalls, the smell of the hay, and the warmth of the stable. Jacob also returned but with a much larger number of sheep than John, yet only a fraction of the flock seemed to recognize their surroundings. These sheep lacked the familiarity with the stalls, the scent of the hay, and the warmth of the stable. Jacob's pride in his accomplishment caused him to be boastful as he reunited with John.

"Surely, the Shepherd will be most pleased with me as I brought more sheep home then you," he stated proudly to John, as the two men looked over their sheep.

"Yes, but many of these sheep you've returned with are not the Shepherd's sheep. I even see some goats mixed in with your sheep," John replied.

Jacob justified himself, "My master will not care that these aren't all his sheep; after all, they are still sheep. He will be pleased that I brought him such a sizable number of them. He will reward me for all my work in gathering so many sheep for him."

John said, "I did my best to bring as many of the Shepherd's sheep home. I remained faithful to the Shepherd's commands and only brought home his sheep."

The two servants retired to their rooms, each believing they had done the right thing which would earn favor in their master's eyes when he returned.

Chapter 7
The Return Of The Shepherd

The day the servants had been waiting so patiently for finally came. The Shepherd returned home. He embraced the two servants and told them about the new land he had acquired - a bigger and better land for all his animals and servants, a place he had been preparing, where they could all live together in peace and prosperity. Once he had finished greeting his servants, the Great Shepherd, filled with anticipation, requested to see his beloved sheep.

As the three men made their way to the sheep's pen, the servants recounted how the sheep had been scattered across different lands during a great storm. Each spoke of their journeys to retrieve the lost sheep and return them safely to their home.

Arriving at the pen, the Great Shepherd's heart filled with happiness as many of the sheep, seeing their Shepherd, leapt for joy, running toward him as fast as their little legs could carry them. The Shepherd knelt down to lovingly pet his sheep who had been waiting patiently for his return.

However, many sheep paid no attention to the Shepherd, for they did not know him. As the Shepherd examined these sheep, a look of confusion clouded his expression. Turning to his servants, he asked, "Some of these sheep I do not know and they do not know me. Did you sing the song I commanded you to sing?"

John, with his head bowed in humility, answered first, "I did exactly as you instructed."

Jacob admitted proudly, "Well, I did at first, but I could only find a few sheep that way. So, instead of just singing your song, I used grains and vegetables to attract the sheep. When I did this, many more sheep followed me. I thought, what does it matter? A sheep is a sheep."

The Shepherd's countenance shifted from concern to firm rebuke.

"I don't know these sheep, and they don't know me. They are not welcome here. Leave here and take them with you."

With a bowed head, Jacob left, burdened with shame, as the Shepherd stood resolute in his commitment to the genuine connection with his true flock.

Chapter 8
The Faithful Servant

The Shepherd turned to John and spoke with a voice filled with gratitude, "Your reward is that you will now be a son to me. Everything that is mine is yours, for you have done what Jacob did not. You brought home my sheep by singing my song. You were faithful to the message and, therefore, faithful to me."

John, humbled by such a tremendous reward, lived the remainder of his days not as a mere servant, but as a beloved son to the great Shepherd.

The Great Shepherd, now standing amidst his flock, raised his voice and sang his song with a heightened intensity, echoing across the landscape.

The sheep, attuned to the familiar melody, found solace under the compassionate care of the gentle Shepherd for the rest of their days.

The Shepherd's Song
Words & Music by Jeffrey T. Small

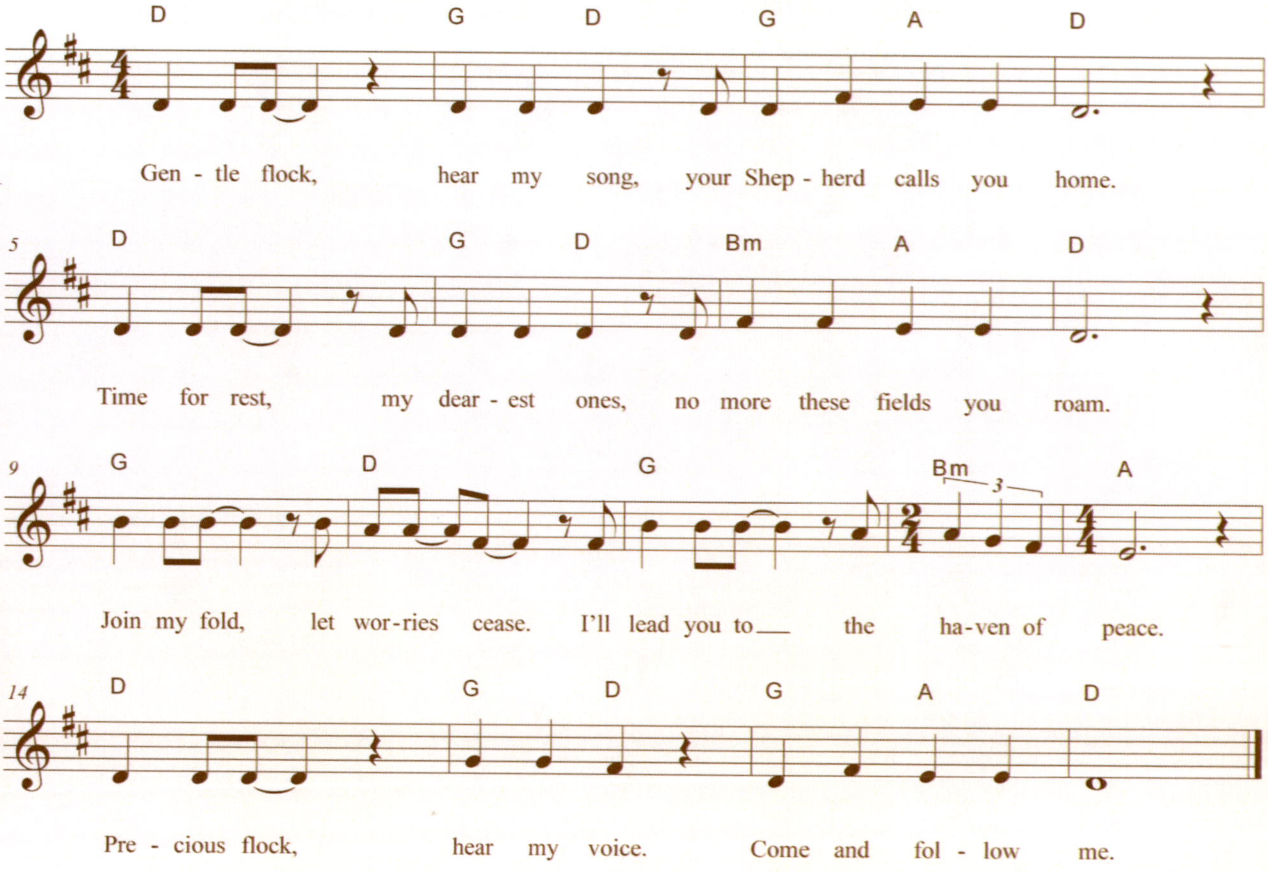

Gen - tle flock, hear my song, your Shep - herd calls you home.

Time for rest, my dear - est ones, no more these fields you roam.

Join my fold, let wor - ries cease. I'll lead you to＿ the ha - ven of peace.

Pre - cious flock, hear my voice. Come and fol - low me.

©2024 Jeffrey T. Small

Epilogue
The Good News

In the Bible, Jesus says in John 10, "I am the good shepherd: the good shepherd gives his life for the sheep. I am the good shepherd, and know my sheep, and my sheep know me. I lay down my life for the sheep. My sheep hear my voice, and I know them, and they follow me: And I give unto them eternal life; and they shall never perish."

Jesus is the Good Shepherd and we are His servants. He commands us to go into all the world and "sing His song" which is another way to say "preach the gospel". The gospel is the message that all who turn from their sins and put their faith in Christ Jesus will be saved (Romans 10:9) and welcomed into his Kingdom (Mark 1:15).

When we preach the gospel and nothing more, His sheep will hear His voice and come to Him. We must not change the gospel or gather sheep by ways other than what He commands us to do.

Sometimes we may feel that our efforts are not being received in the way we hoped they would be. For many will hear the gospel and not believe but it is because they are not His sheep. Still, we must not get discouraged but remain faithful to the message and faithful to the Shepherd, trusting that His sheep WILL hear His voice and come.

May we, like John, always remain faithful servants as we journey together in this world singing The Shepherd's Song.

Printed in the USA
CPSIA information can be obtained
at www.ICGtesting.com
LVRC090451291024
794799LV00010B/173